WE EMPOWER

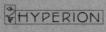

HYPERION

NEW YORK

WE EMPOWER

INSPIRATIONAL WISDOM FOR WOMEN

Introduction by MARIA SHRIVER

ISBN: 978-1-4013-0982-4

Hyperion books are available for special promotions, premiums, or corporate training. For details contact Michael Rentas, Proprietary Markets, Hyperion, 77 West 66th Street, 12th floor, New York, New York 10023, or call 212-456-0133.

BOOK DESIGN BY SHUBHANI SARKAR

FIRST EDITION

10 9 8 7 6 5 4 3 2 1

WE EMPOWER

Words have power—the power to inspire and guide us, touch our hearts, even change the way we look at our lives. A great idea well-expressed can give voice to our innermost yearnings or illuminate the path to our fulfillment.

So I try to start every day by reading a page from one of the many inspirational books I have—or I read one of the hundreds of quotations I've collected through the years, bits of wisdom I've read or heard that have moved or motivated me.

Some of the readings calm me down. Others fire me up and get me going. They may inspire me to dig down deep into myself and get in touch with strength I sometimes don't know I have. Sitting quietly just a moment with the meaning of the words helps me go out into the world to accomplish, achieve, connect with others, and stay true to myself.

Since taking over the California Governor and First Lady's Conference on Women in 2004, I've invited scores of speakers to come and inspire us—people I admire who have walked their own paths, faced hardships, and triumphed. I ask them to write down a great thought or idea, a "tip" they can share on how to live rewarding and productive lives, raise happy children, have strong and loving relationships, rise above our limitations, take risks, overcome obstacles, and fulfill our dreams.

Each year we've collected these "tips" into a little book, and it's become a big hit. This year, we're passing the tips on to you, too.

So if you need a little inspiration to spark your day, please pick up this book, open it at random, and read the quotation you find there. If that one doesn't hit the spot, keep flipping through until you find the perfect words that give you what you need: a shot of courage or encouragement, a jolt of insight or empowerment, a key to your own willingness and wisdom.

And if the tip does the trick—pass it on!

Maria Shriver

Try to live an authentic life that feels true to yourself—which means living as yourself, not an imitation of anyone else, and not the reflection of yourself in anyone else's eyes.

MARIA SHRIVER

FIRST LADY OF CALIFORNIA

. . . .

I f you are in search of wisdom, clarity, help, or love, consider inspiration from sources centered on Divine Will.

SISTER ANDREA JAEGER

PHILANTHROPIST &
FORMER U.S. PROFESSIONAL TENNIS PLAYER

· ·

Take a stand. Be known for your courage and confidence.

INDRA NOOYI

CHAIRMAN & CEO, PEPSICO

. . . .

*B*e *optimistic.* Too often, cynicism can be the fellow traveler of learning.

CONDOLEEZZA RICE

UNITED STATES SECRETARY OF STATE

. . . .

I t's never too late to become the person you have always wanted to be.

ANNE SWEENEY

CO-CHAIR, DISNEY MEDIA NETWORKS &
PRESIDENT, DISNEY-ABC TELEVISION GROUP

· · · · · · · · · · · · · · · · · · ·

Be true to yourself.

CHERIE BLAIR

HUMAN RIGHTS ADVOCATE
& WIFE OF FORMER PRIME MINISTER TONY BLAIR

. . . .

The first step to success for women and girls is to learn how to interrupt. In the classroom or workplace, a woman who is afraid to interrupt may never be heard, and only by being heard can we make a difference.

MADELEINE K. ALBRIGHT

FORMER U.S. SECRETARY OF STATE

Y ou have sole custody of your life. Who you are today is not who you have to be tomorrow. Embrace the possibility of transformation.

LEEZA GIBBONS

TELEVISION & RADIO PRODUCER, HOST
CO-FOUNDER & BOARD CHAIR,
THE LEEZA GIBBONS MEMORY FOUNDATION

The Rolling Stones were wrong—time isn't on your side. But if you do it right, you'll have exactly enough time for the important things in life.

NANCY MCFADDEN

SENIOR VICE PRESIDENT, PUBLIC AFFAIRS, PG&E CORPORATION

. . . .

W hatever one aspires to be can be realized if one is rooted on a foundation of ethics, fair play, and honesty.

DEBORAH NORVILLE

ANCHOR, *INSIDE EDITION* & AUTHOR, *THANK YOU POWER*

Be an example for others even (especially) when no one is looking.

LAURA SCHULTE

PRESIDENT, WESTERN REGION, WELLS FARGO

. . . .

We come to our understanding of God, our sense of the sacred, through the stories of our lives. As you grapple with the raw materials of your days, be a theologian.

KRISTA TIPPETT

HOST, PUBLIC RADIO'S *SPEAKING OF FAITH*

. . . .

The most important thing is for you to go deep down inside and to ask yourself, "What do *I* want to accomplish? Where do *I* want to go?" Not what *someone else* wants you to do.

ARNOLD SCHWARZENEGGER

GOVERNOR OF CALIFORNIA

B e persistent. There are a thousand ways for people to tell you "no," and it's up to you to figure out the "yes."

HEIDI KLUM

HOST & EXECUTIVE PRODUCER, *PROJECT RUNWAY*,
SUPERMODEL & ENTREPRENEUR

. . . .

When you feel hopeless and decide not to go, fight that dragon. Chest out, pumps on, out the door woman.

GISELLE FERNANDEZ

TELEVISION JOURNALIST, PRODUCER & FILMMAKER

. . . .

Change is in your DNA. You are born with a change muscle, an innate ability to make and face any change.

ARIANE DE BONVOISIN

AUTHOR, *THE FIRST 30 DAYS: YOUR GUIDE TO ANY CHANGE*

Sharing your own inspirational story can spark a collective awakening around the world.

JENNY MCCARTHY

BEST-SELLING AUTHOR, ACTRESS & MOTHER

. . . .

Develop a system for living your life. Using a system will avoid omitting important elements of the equation needed to calculate success.

DR. MEHMET OZ

HEALTH EXPERT, *THE OPRAH WINFREY SHOW*
& CO-AUTHOR OF THE "YOU" SERIES HEALTH BOOKS WITH
LISA OZ AND DR. MIKE ROIZEN

. . . .

Keep your honor.

TIM RUSSERT

FORMER MODERATOR, *MEET THE PRESS*
WOMEN'S CONFERENCE, 2006

. . . .

As you juggle life's balls, remember that some are crystal and some plastic.

DEBORAH ROBERTS

ABC NEWS CORRESPONDENT

. . . .

Styles, like everything else, change. Style doesn't.

LINDA ELLERBEE

JOURNALIST, AUTHOR & TELEVISION PRODUCER

. . . .

WE EMPOWER

We have the technology, the smarts in global health, in agriculture, and in commerce to dramatically improve the quality and longevity of the one billion lives that live on one dollar a day or less. We can't fix every problem but the ones we can we must.

BONO

LEAD SINGER OF U2
AND CO-FOUNDER OF THE ANTI-POVERTY CAMPAIGN ONE

· · · · · · · ·

We tend to keep our dark secrets, but openness is a relief. We're no longer alone in our suffering.

DAVID SHEFF

AUTHOR, *BEAUTIFUL BOY*

· · · · · · · · · · · · · · · · ·

W

hatever you do, do not sit on the sidelines of life! Self-absorbed is so *yesterday*!

CHRISTIANE AMANPOUR

CHIEF INTERNATIONAL CORRESPONDENT, CNN

. . . .

N

ever give up! There's always *hope*— because there's always *help*.

SUSAN FORD BALES

CHAIRMAN, BETTY FORD CENTER

. . . .

Life is not about traveling through. Life is about doing something to bring the world one step closer to completion.

SISTER JOAN CHITTISTER, OSB

AUTHOR, *THE GIFT OF YEARS*

. . . .

Within you is the power to do anything . . . with confidence and inspiration, you unlock the possibilities.

KRISTIN GIBBS

DIRECTOR OF MARKETING, LEAN CUISINE

. . . .

P

ossibly, the only thing that can bring as much peace of mind as the truth is knowing you have done all you can to find it.

MARY TILLMAN

AUTHOR, *BOOTS ON THE GROUND BY DUSK:*
MY TRIBUTE TO PAT TILLMAN

. . . .

You can't be all things to all people, so don't even try.

RACHAEL RAY

DAYTIME HOST

. . . .

WE EMPOWER

D
on't be scared to present the "real you" to the world—authenticity is at the heart of success.

CHIQUI CARTAGENA

AUTHOR, HISPANIC EXPERT &
MANAGING DIRECTOR OF INTEGRATED MARKETING AT
MEREDITH HISPANIC VENTURES

I f the market scares you, use fear to your advantage. Without investigating, you won't be able to retire comfortably, help your children with their college tuition, or cover a medical emergency.

JEAN CHATZKY

BEST-SELLING AUTHOR, *MAKE MONEY, NOT EXCUSES* & FINANCIAL EDITOR FOR NBC'S *TODAY*

. . . .

Serving with and for those in need, you
will answer the call to action for social justice,
and you will change lives. You will change
the world.

EUNICE KENNEDY SHRIVER

2007 MINERVA LIFETIME ACHIEVEMENT AWARD WINNER

. . . .

As women we have the opportunity to lift up other women through words, deeds, and intentions.

JESS WEINER

AUTHOR / SELF-ESTEEM EXPERT

. . . .

Ask! Don't say no to yourself. Make the other person say no.

CHRIS MATTHEWS

HOST OF *HARDBALL* ON MSNBC
AND *THE CHRIS MATTHEWS SHOW* ON NBC

. . . .

Every morning, ask yourself not "What do I need to DO today?" but "How do I need to BE today?" Focus on how you can be YOUR authentic, best self.

SHANNON MCFAYDEN

SENIOR EXECUTIVE VICE PRESIDENT, WACHOVIA CORPORATION

WE EMPOWER

Edit your e-mail every Friday afternoon. Unplug, tune out every Saturday. Clean out your purse and wallet every Sunday.

SARAH BAN BREATHNACH

AUTHOR, *SIMPLE ABUNDANCE:
A DAYBOOK OF COMFORT AND JOY*

Accept each moment as if you had chosen it. That frees you of all negativity. Then take action and do what you have to do.

ECKHART TOLLE

AUTHOR & SPIRITUAL TEACHER

. . . .

Most of our stress and suffering comes not from events, but from our thoughts. Reframe negative thoughts, and stress subsides.

MARTHA BECK, PH.D.

LIFE COACH

. . . .

Do not compare yourself to others. You have a unique destiny and mission that only you can accomplish.

MARIANE PEARL

AUTHOR, WIFE OF JOURNALIST DANIEL PEARL

. . . .

Use romantic relationships to grow, not to lose yourself. Keep your priorities in order.

TYRA BANKS

HOST, *AMERICA'S NEXT TOP MODEL* & *THE TYRA BANKS SHOW*

. . . .

Lesson number one: Take risks, look for gaps, and do what no one else is doing.

MICHAEL J. FOX

ACTOR, AUTHOR & FOUNDER OF
THE MICHAEL J. FOX FOUNDATION FOR PARKINSON'S RESEARCH

. . . .

Judge your success not just by what you have accomplished, but by the person you have become.

RANJANA CLARK

CHIEF MARKETING OFFICER, WACHOVIA CORPORATION

. . . .

Seek diversity in your experiences and continue learning.

LAURA K. IPSEN

SENIOR VICE PRESIDENT,
GLOBAL POLICY AND GOVERNMENT AFFAIRS, CISCO

. . . .

WE EMPOWER

S pend a little time outdoors each day in gratitude for your life and all that is in it.

RITA WILSON

ACTOR, PRODUCER

. . . .

Women are a voice for the voiceless.

CERUE KONAH GARLO

EXECUTIVE DIRECTOR,
WOMEN NGOS SECRETARIAT OF LIBERIA (WONGOSOL)

Awoman should always be more concerned with standing up for what is right than making sure everyone "likes" her.

DR. LAURA SCHLESSINGER

RADIO TALK SHOW HOST & AUTHOR

On *Success*—What you DO is not who you ARE. Success is not to be determined by the people around you. Being in this business I have decided I won't allow people to determine what MY success is. My biggest success may be raising children and having a successful marriage and not how many records I sell or how many movies I make.

KATHARINE MCPHEE

RCA RECORDING ARTIST

Leadership—be passionate, consistent, and truthful. Surround yourself with the right people. Have an open mind and a kind disposition.

ISABEL ALLENDE

AUTHOR, *THE HOUSE OF THE SPIRITS*

Life is a series of challenges. How well you face them is how well you live your life.

CINDY HENSLEY MCCAIN

CHAIRMAN, HENSLEY & COMPANY

. . . .

Be fearless. Every great idea that changed the world came from someone who was brave enough to call for it.

SYLVIA BOORSTEIN, PH.D.

CO-FOUNDER & TEACHER, SPIRIT ROCK MEDITATION CENTER

Luck is when opportunity meets preparedness.

CHRISTINE TODD WHITMAN

FORMER GOVERNOR OF NEW JERSEY

Give yourself the same compassion you extend to others.

BONNIE RAITT

SINGER, SONGWRITER & GUITARIST

. . . .

Meditation—through stillness you will find the strength you didn't know you had is just sitting inside you, waiting to be utilized.

RUSSELL SIMMONS

CHAIRMAN, RUSH COMMUNICATIONS

. . . .

To watch how lovingly your children parent their own children is to know profound achievement.

SALLY FIELD

ACTOR

. . . .

Persistence and passion are the ingredients you need to make dreams come true.

WILLIAM G. MARGARITIS

SENIOR VICE PRESIDENT, GLOBAL COMMUNICATIONS &
INVESTOR RELATIONS, FEDEX CORPORATION

　WE EMPOWER

Many issues could be solved by the acceptance of differences—which is tolerance.

CECILIA CIGANER-ATTIAS

CEO, THE EXPERIENCE CORP (USA)

Pray early and pray often; hug early and hug often; laugh early and laugh often. They're all good for your mind, good for your soul, and good for your abs.

TIMOTHY SHRIVER

CHAIRMAN & CEO, SPECIAL OLYMPICS

· ·

Create your legacy, and pass the baton.

BILLIE JEAN KING

CO-FOUNDER, WORLD TEAM TENNIS & WIMBLEDON CHAMPION

. . . .

Embrace change. Don't let fear of the unknown impede your personal and professional growth.

LARREE RENDA

EXECUTIVE VICE PRESIDENT, CHIEF STRATEGIST
& CHIEF ADMINISTRATIVE OFFICER, SAFEWAY

. . . .

My favorite quote is "Only that which changes remains true" —Carl Jung.

JAMIE LEE CURTIS

ACTRESS & AUTHOR

. . . .

As women, we cannot afford to neglect ourselves.

MICHELLE OBAMA

. . . .

WE EMPOWER

Laugh often.

TIM RUSSERT

FORMER MODERATOR, *MEET THE PRESS*
WOMEN'S CONFERENCE, 2006

. . . .

When people don't want the best for you, they ARE NOT the best for you.

GAYLE KING

EDITOR-AT-LARGE, *O, THE OPRAH MAGAZINE*

. . . .

K

eep your priorities straight.

LAURA SCHULTE

PRESIDENT, WESTERN REGION, WELLS FARGO

. . . .

Sometimes, the best way to make a big difference is adding up lots of small ones.

HER MAJESTY

QUEEN RANIA AL ABDULLAH OF JORDAN

Instead of thinking "Why me??" think "Why *not* me? Who am I not to make a difference?"

GISELLE FERNANDEZ

TELEVISION JOURNALIST, PRODUCER & FILMMAKER

. . . .

Eat food that comes out of the ground looking the same as when you eat it.

DR. MEHMET OZ

HEALTH EXPERT, *THE OPRAH WINFREY SHOW*
& CO-AUTHOR OF THE "YOU" SERIES HEALTH BOOKS WITH
LISA OZ AND DR. MIKE ROIZEN

I believe the secret to life is show up, do your best, and then let go of the rest.

LEEZA GIBBONS

TELEVISION & RADIO PRODUCER, HOST
CO-FOUNDER & BOARD CHAIR,
THE LEEZA GIBBONS MEMORY FOUNDATION

. . . .

Change doesn't have to be huge, but it may have to be deep. A deep change for me was realizing I'd have to take the time to know what I feel, in order to know who I am and who I want to be.

MARIA SHRIVER

FIRST LADY OF CALIFORNIA

. . . .

WE EMPOWER

Build knowledge in one key area and become an expert in it. You need a hip-pocket skill.

INDRA NOOYI

CHAIRMAN & CEO, PEPSICO

Our worst mistake is underestimating ourselves and underestimating Life.

ARIANE DE BONVOISIN

AUTHOR, *THE FIRST 30 DAYS: YOUR GUIDE TO ANY CHANGE*

As my mom used to say: "Don't cry over anything that can't cry over you."

MAUREEN DOWD

COLUMNIST, *NEW YORK TIMES* & AUTHOR

The plane is not going to crash.

NORA EPHRON

WRITER & DIRECTOR

. . . .

Buy yourself flowers whenever you can. You deserve it.

DEBORAH ROBERTS

ABC NEWS CORRESPONDENT

. . . .

Nurture your hopes by reading or listening to those who inspire you. Try in turn to inspire those around you.

MARIANE PEARL

AUTHOR, WIFE OF JOURNALIST DANIEL PEARL

. . . .

Let go of the past. If you carry it around like luggage, you won't be able to move forward.

CHIQUI CARTAGENA

AUTHOR, HISPANIC EXPERT &
MANAGING DIRECTOR OF INTEGRATED MARKETING AT
MEREDITH HISPANIC VENTURES

. . . .

Don't wait for someone or something else to come along and provide your happiness. Ultimately, if you're taking actions to enrich your own life and live it to the max, it's best both for yourself and those around you.

HEIDI KLUM

HOST & EXECUTIVE PRODUCER, *PROJECT RUNWAY*,
SUPERMODEL & ENTREPRENEUR

. . . .

WE EMPOWER

Don't be afraid to negotiate at work. Getting what you're worth, as long as you have the conversation appropriately, is the polite thing to do.

JEAN CHATZKY

BEST-SELLING AUTHOR, *MAKE MONEY, NOT EXCUSES* & FINANCIAL EDITOR FOR NBC'S *TODAY*

. . . .

Just because we are not guaranteed success does not mean that we are pardoned the obligation to try.

SISTER JOAN CHITTISTER, OSB

AUTHOR, *THE GIFT OF YEARS*

Your personal reputation is the most important asset in achieving personal success.

WILLIAM G. MARGARITIS

SENIOR VICE PRESIDENT, GLOBAL COMMUNICATIONS &
INVESTOR RELATIONS, FEDEX CORPORATION

. . . .

If an opportunity scares you, that's God's way of saying you should jump at it.

ANNA QUINDLEN

COLUMNIST & AUTHOR

Don't be afraid of your own strength.

DIANE VON FURSTENBERG

FASHION DESIGNER & PRESIDENT,
COUNCIL OF FASHION DESIGNERS OF AMERICA

Don't listen to experts if your gut tells you something is wrong with their advice.

MARY TILLMAN

AUTHOR, *BOOTS ON THE GROUND BY DUSK:
MY TRIBUTE TO PAT TILLMAN*

. . . .

WE EMPOWER

There are two kinds of fun: Fun that thrills and fun that lasts. Have both, but know the difference.

TIMOTHY SHRIVER

CHAIRMAN & CEO, SPECIAL OLYMPICS

My mother {Betty Ford} said it best: "Secrets can be poison. Better, almost always, to say what needs to be said."

SUSAN FORD BALES

CHAIRMAN, BETTY FORD CENTER

Always be willing to disappoint another to be true to yourself; that is a true leader and architect for change.

JESS WEINER

AUTHOR / SELF-ESTEEM EXPERT

. . . .

I used to hate my body. Some days I still do. I think learning to love ourselves is an ongoing process. The key for me was finally confronting the real issues at hand—what is going on "inside." Fixing ourselves from the inside out and finding the source of our insecurity eventually leads us away from fixating on things such as our bodies.

KATHARINE MCPHEE

RCA RECORDING ARTIST

For every promise you make to others, keep one to yourself.

SARAH BAN BREATHNACH

AUTHOR, *SIMPLE ABUNDANCE:*
A DAYBOOK OF COMFORT AND JOY

Your personal history is not your true identity. Don't let the past define who you are, which is consciousness itself, the "light of the world."

ECKHART TOLLE

AUTHOR & SPIRITUAL TEACHER

. . . .

I

t's not the balanced life we remember,
it's the beautiful life.

ANNE SWEENEY

CO-CHAIR, DISNEY MEDIA NETWORKS &
PRESIDENT, DISNEY-ABC TELEVISION GROUP

. . . .

The minute you settle for less than you deserve, you get even less than you settled for.

MAUREEN DOWD

COLUMNIST, *NEW YORK TIMES* & AUTHOR

. . . .

Perfect is boring. In recognizing our flaws,
we find what makes us interesting.

TYRA BANKS

HOST, *AMERICA'S NEXT TOP MODEL* & *THE TYRA BANKS SHOW*

. . . .

We, as women, cannot afford to allow someone else to neglect us.

MICHELLE OBAMA

· · · · · · · · · · · · · · · · · · · ·

Give yourself permission to leave the dishes in the sink.

LEE WOODRUFF

AUTHOR, *IN AN INSTANT*

. . . .

We are living in a deluded state. The only thing that can shatter that delusion is truth and the courage to change.

JAMIE LEE CURTIS

ACTRESS & AUTHOR

No material object, however beautiful or valuable, can make us feel loved, because our deeper identity and true character lie in the subjective nature of the mind.

HIS HOLINESS THE DALAI LAMA

Call yourself a feminist. Proudly. But remember: Men are not the enemy and women aren't the only solution. We're all flying on this planet together.

LYNN SHERR

CORRESPONDENT, *20/20*, ABC NEWS
& AUTHOR, *OUTSIDE THE BOX: A MEMOIR*

. . . .

WE EMPOWER

The pages of your life belong to you. Write a story that makes you happy and proud. And someday, somewhere, a wonderful little girl will read it and say, "I want to be just like her."

HER MAJESTY

QUEEN RANIA AL ABDULLAH OF JORDAN

Studies have proven that afternoon napping has great health benefits. Morning, therefore, probably isn't such a bad idea either . . .

ELIZABETH GILBERT

AUTHOR, *EAT, PRAY, LOVE*

WE EMPOWER

Everybody has a story that is just as important as your own; therefore, you are no better and no worse than anyone you will ever meet.

GAYLE KING

EDITOR-AT-LARGE, *O, THE OPRAH MAGAZINE*

. . . .

When you really want to say no, say no. You can't do everything—or at least not well.

ANNA QUINDLEN

COLUMNIST & AUTHOR

. . . .

WE EMPOWER

Every day try to be a blessing to everyone you meet.

BONNIE RAITT

SINGER, SONGWRITER & GUITARIST

We are not any better a person simply by describing someone else as worse.

ELIZABETH EDWARDS

AUTHOR, *SAVING GRACES*

. . . .

Life is short—insecurity is a waste of time.

DIANE VON FURSTENBERG

FASHION DESIGNER & PRESIDENT,
COUNCIL OF FASHION DESIGNERS OF AMERICA

Every era has its defining struggles and the fate of Africa is one of ours. Africa is this generation's proving ground for whether we truly believe in the concept of equality, or not . . . Where you live should not decide whether you live or whether you die.

BONO

LEAD SINGER OF U2
AND CO-FOUNDER OF THE ANTI-POVERTY CAMPAIGN ONE

. . . .

Whatever you do in your life, think higher, feel deeper.

CECILIA CIGANER-ATTIAS

CEO, THE EXPERIENCE CORP (USA)

. . . .

Stop thinking or acting like life will happen *after* everything is crossed off your list.

NANCY MCFADDEN

SENIOR VICE PRESIDENT, PUBLIC AFFAIRS, PG&E CORPORATION

· ·

Aim high, focus your energies, and color everything you do with a sense of urgency.

MICHAEL J. FOX

ACTOR, AUTHOR & FOUNDER OF
THE MICHAEL J. FOX FOUNDATION FOR PARKINSON'S RESEARCH

We all stand on the shoulders of women who came before us. Make sure yours are strong enough to support the women who will come after you.

LINDA ELLERBEE

JOURNALIST, AUTHOR & TELEVISION PRODUCER

. . . .

WE EMPOWER

Define success on your own terms, achieve it by your own rules, and build a life you're proud to live.

ANNE SWEENEY

CO-CHAIR, DISNEY MEDIA NETWORKS &
PRESIDENT, DISNEY-ABC TELEVISION GROUP

. . . .

*F*ind and follow your passion. As you work to find it, you should know that sometimes, your passion just finds you.

CONDOLEEZZA RICE

UNITED STATES SECRETARY OF STATE

. . . .

The last thing you expect or want in life is often the first thing to take you on your journey to life.

TIMOTHY SHRIVER

CHAIRMAN & CEO, SPECIAL OLYMPICS

. . . .

Go into everything believing it will work.

JENNY MCCARTHY

BEST-SELLING AUTHOR, ACTRESS & MOTHER

. . . .

In every job, in every assignment, in every situation, look for ways to expand your knowledge.

RANJANA CLARK

CHIEF MARKETING OFFICER, WACHOVIA CORPORATION

W

omen are the radiance of peace in every nation.

CERUE KONAH GARLO

EXECUTIVE DIRECTOR,
WOMEN NGOS SECRETARIAT OF LIBERIA (WONGOSOL)

. . . .

Start to think of your spiritual questions, not just your answers, as blessed and sacred.

KRISTA TIPPETT

HOST, PUBLIC RADIO'S *SPEAKING OF FAITH*

. . . .

Think beyond limitations. My mother, shorter than I am, said, "Wear whatever you want. You will determine the style."

SYLVIA BOORSTEIN, PH.D.

CO-FOUNDER & TEACHER, SPIRIT ROCK MEDITATION CENTER

Set personal goals that exceed those set for you by others.

LARREE RENDA

EXECUTIVE VICE PRESIDENT, CHIEF STRATEGIST
& CHIEF ADMINISTRATIVE OFFICER, SAFEWAY

. . . .

*O*ne of the secrets to a long life is to stay in school. When it comes to health and longevity, education is more important than race or income. So regardless of your age, never stop learning.

DR. NANCY L. SNYDERMAN

CHIEF MEDICAL EDITOR, NBC NEWS & LLUMINARI EXPERT

If you can answer one question, you will know how to answer all the others: "Who am I?" When you know the answer to this, you know the answer to all other questions.

DEBORAH NORVILLE

ANCHOR, *INSIDE EDITION* & AUTHOR, *THANK YOU POWER*

I f you insist on thinking yourself a sausage, at least think chicken link. We project what we think, what we hope.

GISELLE FERNANDEZ

TELEVISION JOURNALIST, PRODUCER & FILMMAKER

. . . .

Don't be modest in your goals.

CHERIE BLAIR

HUMAN RIGHTS ADVOCATE
& WIFE OF FORMER PRIME MINISTER TONY BLAIR

. . . .

Life is sweetened by risk, so dare to dream big and get comfortable with being uncomfortable. It's only by stepping outside of our safety zone that we truly grow.

LEEZA GIBBONS

TELEVISION & RADIO PRODUCER, HOST
CO-FOUNDER & BOARD CHAIR,
THE LEEZA GIBBONS MEMORY FOUNDATION

What I've come to understand is that we are first and foremost human beings in our own right. We're entitled to our own lives, our own dreams and goals, our own legacies.

MARIA SHRIVER

FIRST LADY OF CALIFORNIA

. . . .

When everything around you is changing, turn to the part of you that doesn't change, that is calm, centered, and connected to something bigger.

ARIANE DE BONVOISIN

AUTHOR, *THE FIRST 30 DAYS: YOUR GUIDE TO ANY CHANGE*

Everything is always an emergency and it will be an emergency tomorrow as well.

RACHAEL RAY

DAYTIME HOST

. . . .

Chart your own course, but embrace the stormy seas.

LAURA K. IPSEN

SENIOR VICE PRESIDENT,
GLOBAL POLICY AND GOVERNMENT AFFAIRS, CISCO

. . . .

WE EMPOWER

Find the thing that ignites your passion, engages your mind, and dare to lead.

CHRISTIANE AMANPOUR

CHIEF INTERNATIONAL CORRESPONDENT, CNN

Compassion and Love—if you want to change the world or one individual, the only way to do it is to love it or them.

RUSSELL SIMMONS

CHAIRMAN, RUSH COMMUNICATIONS

....

Remember: You're not alone.

JUDITH WARNER

AUTHOR, *PERFECT MADNESS: MOTHERHOOD IN THE AGE OF ANXIETY*

I've only watched my feet as I've moved through life and am amazed to see the distance I've traveled.

SALLY FIELD

ACTOR

· · · · · · · · · · · · · · · ·

WE EMPOWER

One can choose to live fully and with success regardless of challenges, circumstances, or environment.

SISTER ANDREA JAEGER

PHILANTHROPIST &
FORMER U.S. PROFESSIONAL TENNIS PLAYER

I f you want to start saving, you have to keep your eyes on the prize. Know what your goal is (Retirement? A vacation? Your first home?) and how much it's going to cost you, then work to get there.

JEAN CHATZKY

BEST-SELLING AUTHOR, *MAKE MONEY, NOT EXCUSES* & FINANCIAL EDITOR FOR NBC'S *TODAY*

. . . .

Work hard.

TIM RUSSERT

FORMER MODERATOR, *MEET THE PRESS*
WOMEN'S CONFERENCE, 2006

. . . .

Honor tradition, but challenge rules that seem outdated, irrelevant, or downright wrong.

SARAH FERGUSON

THE DUCHESS OF YORK

. . . .

WE EMPOWER

The most important steps toward change are the small ones.

JESS WEINER

AUTHOR / SELF-ESTEEM EXPERT

. . . .

Be strong. Go after your goal. It's going to be a big struggle and a lot of work. And make sure that you understand one thing; that you are the only obstacle.

ARNOLD SCHWARZENEGGER

GOVERNOR OF CALIFORNIA

Be fearless in trying new things, whether they are physical, mental, or emotional, since being afraid can challenge you to go to the next level.

RITA WILSON

ACTOR, PRODUCER

. . . .

R aising children is one of life's greatest adventures. Enjoy every twist and turn in the road.

WILLOW BAY

BROADCAST JOURNALIST

. . . .

If you linger on the past, you can never move forward. Holding grudges, believing that people never change or that you can't change yourself, you will never progress in your life.

RAVEN-SYMONÉ

ACTRESS

. . . .

Get "out of your mind" to get into your right life.

MARTHA BECK, PH.D.

LIFE COACH

When you've gotten really good at your job, change it or leave it.

ANNA QUINDLEN

COLUMNIST & AUTHOR

. . . .

What would you attempt to do if you knew you could not fail?

ELLE MACPHERSON

FOUNDER & CHAIR, ELLE MACPHERSON INTIMATES

. . . .

People first. Then money. Then things. That is the correct order of wealth.

SUZE ORMAN

FINANCE EXPERT, AUTHOR & HOST, *THE SUZE ORMAN SHOW*, CNBC

. . . .

Let's lay to rest the tired old stereotype of the suffering artist. Creativity exists to sustain us, not to torment us.

ELIZABETH GILBERT

AUTHOR, *EAT, PRAY, LOVE*

. . . .

Find your passion, learn about it, make it your own, and then others will follow.

CHRISTINE TODD WHITMAN

FORMER GOVERNOR OF NEW JERSEY

Anything you think is wrong with your body at the age of 35, you will be nostalgic for at the age of 45.

NORA EPHRON

WRITER & DIRECTOR

. . . .

WE EMPOWER

Accumulate wisdom, not baggage.
The lighter you travel, the farther and higher
you can go.

SARAH FERGUSON

THE DUCHESS OF YORK

. . . .

Quality is something you should strive for in every decision, every day.

MARTHA STEWART

FOUNDER, MARTHA STEWART LIVING OMNIMEDIA

. . . .

Hold on to your ideals. Sometimes it is important to lose for things that matter.

MARIAN WRIGHT EDELMAN

FOUNDER & CEO, CHILDREN'S DEFENSE FUND

From the Greek Epictetus: "Ask not that events should happen as you will—but let your will be that events should happen, and you will have peace."

DEBORAH NORVILLE

ANCHOR, *INSIDE EDITION* & AUTHOR, *THANK YOU POWER*

· ·

Exchange the words "have to" with "get to." Exchange the word "can't" with "unwilling."

JAMIE LEE CURTIS

ACTRESS & AUTHOR

. . . .

Face your fears; live your passions; be dedicated to your truth.

BILLIE JEAN KING

CO-FOUNDER, WORLD TEAM TENNIS & WIMBLEDON CHAMPION

. . . .

W hen life seems overwhelming, take things an hour at a time—find comfort in the little triumphs.

LEE WOODRUFF

AUTHOR, *IN AN INSTANT*

. . . .

Give your kids time to dream.

JUDITH WARNER

AUTHOR, *PERFECT MADNESS: MOTHERHOOD IN THE AGE OF ANXIETY*

. . . .

We can try to protect our children, but they must choose if and how to live. We can, however, always love them.

DAVID SHEFF

AUTHOR, *BEAUTIFUL BOY*

. . . .

More women in decision making means less corruption, more development and stability.

CERUE KONAH GARLO

EXECUTIVE DIRECTOR,
WOMEN NGOS SECRETARIAT OF LIBERIA (WONGOSOL)

. . . .

Listening is becoming a lost art—practice it.

NANCY MCFADDEN

SENIOR VICE PRESIDENT, PUBLIC AFFAIRS, PG&E CORPORATION

You should be smart enough to find people who are smarter than you and keep them close. (I found this distressingly easy.)

MICHAEL J. FOX

ACTOR, AUTHOR & FOUNDER OF
THE MICHAEL J. FOX FOUNDATION FOR PARKINSON'S RESEARCH

. . . .

As my father taught me: Assume positive intent in others. When you assume positive intent, you listen better and promote mutual understanding.

INDRA NOOYI

CHAIRMAN & CEO, PEPSICO

. . . .

Be kind to everyone. You'd be surprised how much people appreciate and remember even small thoughtful actions, and how it gets repaid to you.

HEIDI KLUM

HOST & EXECUTIVE PRODUCER, *PROJECT RUNWAY*,
SUPERMODEL & ENTREPRENEUR

. . . .

It's not who you know. It's who you get to know.

CHRIS MATTHEWS

HOST OF *HARDBALL* ON MSNBC
AND *THE CHRIS MATTHEWS SHOW* ON NBC

. . . .

Conquer your fears by working through them because you will never be able to get around them.

CHIQUI CARTAGENA

AUTHOR, HISPANIC EXPERT &
MANAGING DIRECTOR OF INTEGRATED MARKETING AT
MEREDITH HISPANIC VENTURES

. . . .

Compassion and tolerance are not a sign of weakness, but a sign of strength.

HIS HOLINESS THE DALAI LAMA

*E*mbrace diversity. Reject prejudices of all sorts and help close the gaps of justice and opportunity that still divide our nation and our world.

CONDOLEEZZA RICE

UNITED STATES SECRETARY OF STATE

. . . .

Authenticity is the most coveted attribute for a brand. People too. So be yourself—consistently.

WILLIAM G. MARGARITIS

SENIOR VICE PRESIDENT, GLOBAL COMMUNICATIONS &
INVESTOR RELATIONS, FEDEX CORPORATION

When you're climbing the corporate ladder in a skirt, keep the view from below in mind. How you treat people below you and beside you is your most important measure of success.

SHANNON MCFAYDEN

SENIOR EXECUTIVE VICE PRESIDENT, WACHOVIA CORPORATION

I'm best in my faith when I realize God is not only there when you're in trouble. He is always there and that's when we should really be connected to our faith . . . Always.

KATHARINE MCPHEE

RECORDING ARTIST, RCA

Not until I was asked to be a mentor did I appreciate the responsibility and gift of being one; you are guiding, helping, and inspiring others to fulfill their dreams.

GRACIELA MEIBAR

VICE PRESIDENT OF GLOBAL DIVERSITY, MATTEL, INC.

· ·

Diet—invest in a diet that lifts you up rather than drags you down. Some people laugh when they hear, "You are what you eat"—it's really not that funny.

RUSSELL SIMMONS

CHAIRMAN, RUSH COMMUNICATIONS

. . . .

Service is the rent each of us pays for living. The only thing that lasts is what is shared with others.

MARIAN WRIGHT EDELMAN

FOUNDER & CEO, CHILDREN'S DEFENSE FUND

Refrain from being too judgmental. You'll often be surprised by what people have to offer.

LISA LING

HOST, NATIONAL GEOGRAPHIC TELEVISION'S *EXPLORER*,
FORMER HOST, ABC'S *THE VIEW*
& SPECIAL CONTRIBUTOR, *THE OPRAH WINFREY SHOW*

. . . .

Stay resolute. Discover how quickly thinking thoughts of kind and compassionate action rescues your mind from despair and inspires courage.

SYLVIA BOORSTEIN, PH.D.

CO-FOUNDER & TEACHER, SPIRIT ROCK MEDITATION CENTER

Care more about how you can help others be successful than how they can help you succeed.

LAURA SCHULTE

PRESIDENT, WESTERN REGION, WELLS FARGO

. . . .

Never be afraid to admit when you don't know something, but always be willing to seek out the answer. A failure only counts if you let it.

CHRISTINE TODD WHITMAN

FORMER GOVERNOR OF NEW JERSEY

Grieve in places the world does not forgive. Rejoice in places the world does not notice. Live with a patience that culture cannot sustain, and with a hope that the world cannot imagine.

KRISTA TIPPETT

HOST, PUBLIC RADIO'S *SPEAKING OF FAITH*

No one is a jerk on purpose.

DR. MEHMET OZ

HEALTH EXPERT, *THE OPRAH WINFREY SHOW*
& CO-AUTHOR OF THE "YOU" SERIES HEALTH BOOKS WITH
LISA OZ AND DR. MIKE ROIZEN

. . . .

Look to your community for help.
Usually, the answer to most of life's problems
is next door.

RACHAEL RAY

DAYTIME HOST

. . . .

Change the world—read to your kids, recycle, stop a friend from telling a racist joke, walk your talk, pray.

GISELLE FERNANDEZ

TELEVISION JOURNALIST, PRODUCER & FILMMAKER

. . . .

Every day take time to do what you know helps to quiet your mind and open your heart. Walk in the mountains, meditate, take time alone, dance, and pray.

JACK KORNFIELD, PH.D.

CO-FOUNDER & TEACHER, SPIRIT ROCK MEDITATION CENTER

I f somebody stretches out a helping hand, don't look to see if it's old, young, male, female, or green, just take the hand.

LINDA ELLERBEE

JOURNALIST, AUTHOR & TELEVISION PRODUCER

D

o well for yourselves, but also consider doing *good* for your community and our world.

CHRISTIANE AMANPOUR

CNN CHIEF INTERNATIONAL CORRESPONDENT

. . . .

Be a strategic partner in life and at work.

LAURA K. IPSEN

SENIOR VICE PRESIDENT,
GLOBAL POLICY AND GOVERNMENT AFFAIRS, CISCO

. . . .

There is no sin in delegating. The sin is trying to do it all.

DEBORAH ROBERTS

ABC NEWS CORRESPONDENT

F

orgive. Don't condone but forgive and move on. It's the very best revenge.

SALLY FIELD

ACTOR

. . . .

Y̶ou are the architect of your actions, words, and voice. What an opportunity for love, truth, and purpose to shine.

SISTER ANDREA JAEGER

PHILANTHROPIST &
FORMER U.S. PROFESSIONAL TENNIS PLAYER

. . . .

We all come with a gift in our hand designed to make life a better place.

SISTER JOAN CHITTISTER, OSB

AUTHOR, *THE GIFT OF YEARS*

WE EMPOWER

If you come upon the opportunity to improve another's life, seize it immediately!

CINDY HENSLEY MCCAIN

CHAIRMAN, HENSLEY & COMPANY

Your body, like a good horse, knows the path to your destiny. When you head off that path, it resists.

MARTHA BECK, PH.D.

LIFE COACH

. . . .

WE EMPOWER

Try to communicate your thoughts and feelings about something IN THE MOMENT THAT IT'S HAPPENING with grace and understanding, so it doesn't linger with you like old broccoli in the fridge. That stinks!

RITA WILSON

ACTOR, PRODUCER

. . . .

When you think something is wrong, you can't always wait for a consensus of those around you before taking action.

MARY TILLMAN

AUTHOR, *BOOTS ON THE GROUND BY DUSK:*
MY TRIBUTE TO PAT TILLMAN

. . . .

Problems—like addiction—cannot just be ignored. They need to be *addressed*. And if the problem involves someone you love, that means it's yours.

SUSAN FORD BALES

CHAIRMAN, BETTY FORD CENTER

Number 1 on your To Do List every day: Gratitude. This brings grace, ease, pleasure, and productivity to your day.

SARAH BAN BREATHNACH

AUTHOR, *SIMPLE ABUNDANCE:*
A DAYBOOK OF COMFORT AND JOY

The more you are able to understand and appreciate someone else's perspective, the more dimension, depth, and texture you ultimately add to your own.

HER MAJESTY

QUEEN RANIA AL ABDULLAH OF JORDAN

I mproving a child's life is the start of changing a nation—volunteer your time freely and often.

CINDY HENSLEY MCCAIN

CHAIRMAN, HENSLEY & COMPANY

Make an issue of everything that will make your children better adults; let everything else go.

ELIZABETH EDWARDS

AUTHOR, *SAVING GRACES*

. . . .

A hero is a person who doesn't count the cost of sacrifice in time, money, and convenience to bring joy and laughter and hope to the infants and children who are hungry, to women who are overpowered, or to families who are ignored.

EUNICE KENNEDY SHRIVER

2007 MINERVA LIFETIME ACHIEVEMENT AWARD WINNER

It doesn't matter whether you are a waitress or a CEO—the question is are you true to yourself, are you improving the quality of life of those you meet and work with, are you a force for good in a world in desperate need?

HER MAJESTY QUEEN NOOR

When you stand on truth, no one can ever knock you down.

JENNY MCCARTHY

BEST-SELLING AUTHOR, ACTRESS & MOTHER

. . . .

Remain focused on who and what are most important in your life. Making a life is more important than making a living.

LARREE RENDA

EXECUTIVE VICE PRESIDENT, CHIEF STRATEGIST
& CHIEF ADMINISTRATIVE OFFICER, SAFEWAY

Forgive yourself and forgive others around you.

RAVEN-SYMONÉ

ACTRESS

. . . .

Find time for you.

CHERIE BLAIR

HUMAN RIGHTS ADVOCATE
& WIFE OF FORMER PRIME MINISTER TONY BLAIR

. . . .

K

indness works. It's like a boomerang:
It always comes back to you, even if not from
the person you gave it to. I choose to be kind.

GAYLE KING

EDITOR-AT-LARGE, *O, THE OPRAH MAGAZINE*

. . . .

<big>P</big>arenting through a crisis is like being a leader in the military—if you fall apart, so will your troops.

LEE WOODRUFF

AUTHOR, *IN AN INSTANT*

. . . .

Be a good listener. One will always benefit more from listening than conjecturing.

LISA LING

HOST, NATIONAL GEOGRAPHIC TELEVISION'S *EXPLORER*,
FORMER HOST, ABC'S *THE VIEW*
& SPECIAL CONTRIBUTOR, *THE OPRAH WINFREY SHOW*

. . . .

Y ou will NEVER regret staying home and raising your children.

JAMIE LEE CURTIS

ACTRESS & AUTHOR

. . . .

Persevere. Just treatment of children and the poor does not and should not depend on the economic and political weather of the moment. Women must create the political climate in California and America to make preventable child suffering morally and politically unacceptable.

MARIAN WRIGHT EDELMAN

FOUNDER & CEO, CHILDREN'S DEFENSE FUND

Activism—work, work, work, but don't expect to see the results, just hope that your grandchildren will benefit from your activism.

ISABEL ALLENDE

AUTHOR, *THE HOUSE OF THE SPIRITS*

. . . .

YOUR "TIPS"